The Conscious Collaboration Pathway™

An Eight-Step Process to Stretch Donor and Social Impact Dollars while Increasing Impact for the Equity Cause You Care About

Sheron Brown, Ph.D.

The Conscious Collaboration Pathway™
*An Eight-Step Process to Stretch Donor and Social Impact Dollars
while Increasing Impact for the Equity Cause You Care About*

ISBN 978-0-9887466-2-6

Sweet Eden by Sheron, LLC

sheron@drsheronbrown.com
727.379.2545

Interior layout – MiniBük, MiniBuk.com

Typefaces: Mercury Office (headlines), Utopia Std (body text)

MiniBük
minibuk.com

Manufactured in the USA by MiniBük®, a reg. trademark of MiniBük, LLC

Advance Praise for *The Conscious Collaboration Pathway*™

As nonprofit leaders, we too often experience a lack of alignment, duplication of efforts, or competition for funds with other organizations with similar or complementary missions. Dr. Sheron Brown reveals a framework for conscious collaboration—one that allows individual organizations to be upfront about their specific objectives while creating faster, more efficient pathways for solving large, societal problems.

While Dr. Brown specifically looks at improving health equity, this framework can be used for other major challenges that nonprofits work tirelessly to address each day. This is a must read for any nonprofit leader and the foundation and for-profit funders who support them who are looking to change the status quo and create measurable impact.

— Lakshmi Shenoy
CEO, Embarc Collective Tampa Bay

Dedication

This book is dedicated to:

The region that welcomed me with love when it was time to start a new chapter in my life.

The region that is thriving in commerce and is wanting to emerge as the jewel of the South for the United States of America to see what health equity looks like.

The almost 150,000 souls working in nonprofits day and night in Tampa Bay's region who are passionate about changing the world through the causes for which they work.

The thousands of funders and donors who give billions every year to support the causes they care about.

Every human being who is working hard to figure out how to make every community, regardless of demographics, a picture of wholeness.

Contents

Introduction

You're not in the burger business. You're in the real estate business.

— Harry J. Sonneborn's character in the movie "The Founder," written by Robert Siegel

☙❧

Why This Book?

Sometimes you learn lessons in books, and sometimes you learn from one line in a movie. That was my experience when watching the 2016 movie, "The Founder." Ray Kroc, played by Michael Keaton, was determining how to make his hamburger business succeed when B. J. Novak's character, Sonneborn, helped him see the situation through a different lens. That line was life changing for me in whatever role I have served in since then. I now check in with myself to ask, "What business am I in?" After more than two decades of bringing people together for development, to change systems for the sake of making lives better, I have become clear about the business I am in, and it is to inspire change for community well-being through collaboration.

During the years I spent in public education—whether developing teachers or school leaders—my focus was on how to make the system better so that students in underserved communities could excel. Some of those questions were: Who needs to be at the table? How do we get them there? And, how do we help them commit to staying through the process?

As I write this book, while in my current role as the executive director of the Tampa Bay Healthcare Collaborative (TBHC), my questions are the same, but the answers need to come from people who find themselves in, or who are assisting people in impoverished conditions; those challenged by substance abuse; families without quality healthcare or access to care; the unemployed; people who experience lack of shelter...and others who face difficult challenges in life. Essentially, the answers are meant to aid human beings referred to as being *underserved* or who are in *vulnerable* populations. Regardless of the social challenge being addressed, the heart of the issue is health equity.

Health (which I also refer to in this book as community health or community well-being) must be strong, stable, and sustainable to create a foundation that improves lives.

In my career experience of providing development to inspire change, here are the truths I've discovered:

1. No one element within a system can change the system by itself.
2. Government is definitely needed to change laws but changed laws alone won't sustain change within a system because there will be a fight to change back.
3. Social sector organizations are absolutely necessary to assist people who need help, but they alone are unable to change the system that created the need.
4. Private sector organizations are undeniably needed to have a stake in system changes because they either operate and/or have strong influence within society's systems.

This book is rooted in those truths.

The purpose of this book is to make the case for multi-sector collaboration and to provide tools that remove the barriers that may hinder sustained efforts. My aim is to show both public and private sectors a practical pathway for how to collaborate more efficiently, and use public and private dollars wisely, to reach more people and sustain exceptional collective impact. Because of my current role and location, I will at times refer to the Tampa Bay region, but if you are reading this book in New York, or California, the concepts still apply.

Establishing a common understanding about collaboration and its importance is how I chose to begin this book. As an educator, I learned to never take common understanding for granted. Uncommon understanding has been the root of many misaligned initiatives.

After achieving a common understanding, this book moves to what all people should know about the importance of health equity for all. Prior to laying out The Conscious Collaboration™ pathway, you'll examine a process known as 'systems thinking' as a means for deepening the common understanding of how health inequities impact all sectors of society.

You'll be provided ways to take action for making systemic change at the end of this book. I am all about action, and that is why I chose to write a short book. I want you to spend a short time reading and then be inspired to act.

Here's a rule I live by: Before I enter any method of formal communication with colleagues, clients, or any other people with whom I interact, I always set an intention. I ask myself what good I want to see happen as a result of the exchange. Depending on the circumstances, I may or may not share my intention with them.

Because you are willing to invest your time with these words, I am willing to fully share everything I have to pour into it. My intention is this: To inspire change for community well-being through our own collaboration with this content, and to learn what you'll do with it.

Thank you for reading. I appreciate you.

Sheron Brown, Ph.D.

The Conscious Collaboration Pathway™

What is Collaboration?

Collaboration is the tool of choice when players wish to achieve together that which cannot be achieved alone.

— Debrah Mashek[1]

ᏣᎥ

Having been an educator in the public school system, whenever I hear someone asking a question about what something is, the part of my brain that is quite literal goes straight to the dictionary. But after years of coaching leaders to improve their work performance and personal well-being, I have come to understand that more than reading Webster's is required. When people ask, "What is _____?" they want more than a definition. They want to know how, who, when, and why. "Why does it look like that?" or "When did it get to be that way?" and "How does it happen?" or "Who first thought of it?"

In this world, humans need contrast to learn. So, to create a clear picture of what collaboration is, begin with its opposite: competition.

---

1 https://www.psychologytoday.com/us/blog/relationships-intimate-and-more/201602/collaboration-its-not-what-you-think

But First, Competition

Competition is a rivalry to be the best. In childhood, it is often taught that to get the best out of people they need to be in competitive environments. Some competition is good—it can be a motivator—but competition has its place. There are times when competition is the ideal choice and other times when competition does more harm than good.

One place where competition is appropriate is when you compete against yourself. For example, when I took up golf, I learned that every time I play, it's only necessary to outdo myself. Although golf is sometimes played in teams, every player truly competes only against themselves. Everyone works to improve their best score. Golf's truth is that the only real person to beat is yourself and your former performances. When I get on the course, I'm always working to improve my game. The last time I played, the last swing I made, the last hole I played are my setpoints.

Off the golf course, when I've worked for the benefit of transforming whole systems, I've seen how competition is not always ideal. While it's true that competition may serve the greater good when life-saving technology is required to develop a cure (or vaccine, as was the case with the COVID-19 pandemic), when it comes to the well-being of human beings who are *disadvantaged, underserved*, or, *vulnerable*, competition is not the best answer.

Systems Incorporate Collaboration

Individuals who are grouped into categories by various entities with power do not choose labels for themselves. There are systems in place that created the circumstances that gained them those titles. What do I mean by 'systems' in this context? I mean multiple elements within an entire ecosystem, all working together, or collaborating, to create intended or unintended outcomes. Systems include people, organizations, traditions, perceptions, and actions rooted in practiced behaviors and policies that are undergirded by beliefs or mental models.

Since systems are at the core of collaborative effort, multiple organizations, multiple actions, and multiple people work together to create outcomes. The intentional act of seeking victory through competition does not serve well in this space. Collaboration is what's needed—specifically conscious, thoughtful, respectful collaboration.

When there is competition, a practice of resource-hoarding can ensue. This unintended consequence can be costly (perhaps even deadly) when the issue is about transforming systems to improve people's lives. "Once collaboration is in place, people are much more trusting of each other, more willing to stretch themselves and more likely to create amazing results."[2] These results can then translate to the improved impact you and others want to see in your communities.

Conscious Collaboration

Collaboration is when multiple individuals or entities engage in shared coordinated effort to achieve a common goal. This collaboration becomes a conscious effort when all parties involved enter the engagement with the intention that the highest good is to be held for all collaborators and those who will benefit from their efforts.

Sometimes, cooperating is confused with collaborating. Cooperating does involve working together, but more so for the sake of mutual benefits. For example, organizations A and B may agree to use similar ideas to instill a concept within their shared market in order to gain increased revenues for both, but they don't share strategies or resources to work together. Yet they'll receive a mutual benefit—and that is increased revenues for both A and B.

Conscious collaboration literally involves mindful and compassionate co-laboring. With conscious collaboration, those organizations, A and B, share a common goal to co-create a strategy where each of them owns different pieces of the strategy while honoring the other's strengths—and then they share the outcome. There may be additional agreements, such as shared data, leveraging assets, or exchanging resources, but each collaborative partnership decides on their specific details in a way that ensures all collaborators enter and exit the collaboration as whole.

Why Conscious Collaboration?

In my role as executive director at the Tampa Bay Healthcare Collaborative (TBHC), I have had the honor to speak to hundreds of nonprofit leaders. What I know is they all care deeply about their causes and the people they serve. They dedicate long hours, and many times have sacrificed aspects of their personal well-being to ensure positive impacts from their work. Many of them have been and are able to demonstrate evidence of how good changes can occur. What I've seen as a negative in the work of these nonprofit employees (in addition to sacrificing their individual well-being, which I've addressed in another book, *The Wellness-Purpose Connection*) much of the positive changes they've effected can be classified as isolated impacts.

A point that we reiterate at TBHC is: "None of us is as smart as all of us." Since the social ills we witness in our communities are the result of systems, the isolated impacts of individual organizations created with their individual goals, and individual Objectives and Key Results (OKRs), will never be enough to eradicate, or even make miniscule, our large and complex societal problems.

Here is some wisdom from the *Stanford Social Innovation Review* (SSIR), a magazine that addresses solutions to humanity's problems: "No single organization is responsible for any major social problem, nor can any single organization cure it. [...] The problem with relying on the isolated impact of individual organizations is further compounded by the isolation of the nonprofit sector. Social problems arise from the interplay of governmental and commercial activities, not only from the behavior of social sector organizations. As a result, complex problems can be solved only by a cross-sector coalition that engages those outside the nonprofit sector."[2]

Hence, collaboration is required.

The type of *working together* matters—as I referenced in the difference between cooperation and collaboration. To ensure there's a common understanding between the intent in this book and readers, here is information about the types of collaboration that tend to happen in the social sector spaces.

What Are the Different Types of Collaboration?

In the realm of addressing social ills through the work of nonprofits, Kania and Kramer (2011)[3] share the following types of collaborations that are most typical:

1. *Funder collaborative*: funders pool some of their financial resources to address the same issue and provide funds to nonprofits; or, funders pool other resources such as time or staff to interact with leaders from multiple sectors. While this is a very important form of collaboration, especially

2   https://ssir.org/articles/entry/collective_impact
3   https://ssir.org/articles/entry/collective_impact

to the receivers of the funds, the related impact still has the potential to be isolated.

2. *Public-private partnership*: government and private sector organizations come together to address a single issue that impacts a particular group of people. This collaboration is good in that the immediate needs of those receiving the services are addressed, however, the root cause of the individuals' problems may not be addressed, and there is a strong potential for the problem to re-emerge.

3. *Multi-stakeholder Initiative*: different organizations agree to work on a similar issue, but do not necessarily align their efforts, nor do they have agreements that hold themselves accountable for impact. They may have some results, but they may not be clear or sustainable.

4. *Social Sector Network*: relationships that are created with the purpose of mainly sharing information to address a certain period for a short versus a sustained period of time. Sometimes written agreements are established, and some impacts occur, but because of the lack of infrastructure, the impact is not sustainable.

The Conscious Collaboration Pathway™

5. *Collective Impact Initiative*: decision makers representing multiple sectors establish a shared roadmap to solve a social problem. The stakeholders use a 'systems thinking' approach to: create mutually reinforcing tactics that each organization can execute in their shared strategy; establish agreements on communication and measurement; and engage an organization apart from their own to manage their arrangement. The results from this type of collaboration are not isolated and are sustainable.

Leaders of organizations are rightly concerned with their livelihood and sustainability and this concern has the potential to fuel competition in a space where it can end up being harmful. Thankfully, there is a model of collaboration espoused by TBHC that allows seemingly competitive organizations to collaborate and still thrive in the creation of collective impacts.

There is value for communities in collaboration—the collective impact type—and it is time to shift our collective actions to invest in it.

Our people. Our time. Our money.

If you are willing, it is possible.

The Conscious Collaboration Pathway™

What is Health Equity?

Health Equity is both the elimination of systemic obstacles and the creation of opportunities for all to be healthy.

— Vanderbilt University Medical Center's
definition of health equity[4]

಄ೞ

Shortly before I started in my role as executive director at TBHC, the board transformed the vision of the organization. It was energizing and one of the main reasons I wanted to be employed in the role. The vision they created was: "Be the leading catalyst to spark movement on health equity in Tampa Bay." That vision resonated with me because I enjoy being a part of true transformation. The other reason the vision resonated with me was because I was drawn to the idea of sparking a movement that would create wholeness for the community. That's how I view health equity—as a sense of wholeness in the community. In the literature, there are several definitions for health equity that are similar.

---

4   https://www.vumc.org/healthequity/health-equity

A widely held definition of health equity, shared by the Robert Wood Johnson Foundation, is: "Health equity means that everyone has a fair and just opportunity to be as healthy as possible. This requires removing obstacles to health such as poverty, discrimination, and their consequences, including powerlessness and lack of access to good jobs with fair pay, quality education and housing, safe environments, and health care."[5]

The barriers to health equity are rooted in a concept called the Social Determinants of Health (SDoH). Simply stated the SDoH are factors created by an individual's social conditions that can be used to indicate whether or not the person has the opportunity to pursue their best health possible.

There are two things to keep in mind. First, the World Health Organization (WHO) defines health as "a state of complete physical, mental and social well-being and not merely the absence of disease or infirmity."[6] Second, the social factors that contribute to an individual's health, along with the corresponding percentages of their contribution levels to one's health, are represented here:

---

5   https://www.rwjf.org/en/library/research/2017/05/what-is-health-equity-.html
6   https://www.publichealth.com.ng/world-health-organizationwho-definition-of-health/

What Goes Into Your Health?

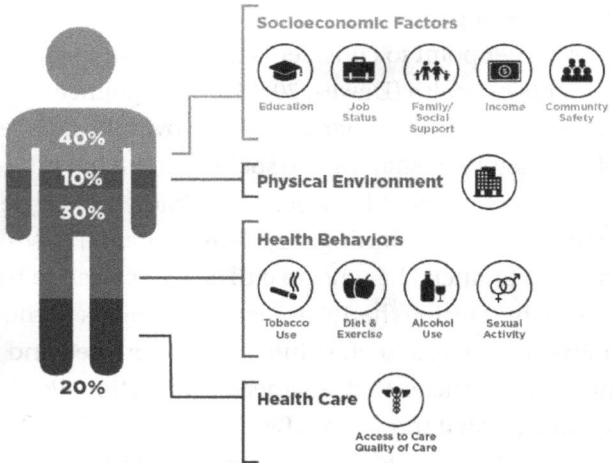

Socioeconomic Factors

Education | Job Status | Family/Social Support | Income | Community Safety

40%
10%
30%

Physical Environment

Health Behaviors

Tobacco Use | Diet & Exercise | Alcohol Use | Sexual Activity

20%

Health Care

Access to Care
Quality of Care

Source: Institute for Clinical Systems Improvement, Going Beyond Clinical Walls: Solving Complex Problems (October 2014)

Adapted from The Bridgespan Group

Unfortunately, it requires more than good hospitals and doctor visits to ensure optimal health. Note that all of these factors contribute to a person's mental well-being. Also unfortunate is that a person's ZIP code can serve as a predictor of their health—it indicates factors such as physical environment, education levels achieved, and community safety. As made clear by the visual, health equity cannot be created with isolated impact. The needle will move only through efforts at collaboration for collective impact.

Another point to consider is the political determinants of health (Dawes, 2020*). What political factors have played a significant role over the course of our history in shaping the social factors that influence a person's health? A clear, well known example is the history of redlining: a systematic denial of social and financial benefits to citizens perceived to be unworthy. During the 1930s, decision makers in the public and private sectors intentionally created and supported policies that advanced segregation. Politicians created those laws. Bankers created those policies. Home builders and nonprofits designed to help the "unfortunates" knowingly or unknowingly supported those detrimental policies through various counteractions—all collaborations that inflicted harm and perpetuated a lack of possibility of achievement, advancement, betterment.

That kind of collaboration contributed to the labels now used for many such as *underserved, disadvantaged, or vulnerable.* Those impacts, still with us today, show up in poor school systems, poor air quality due to dumping in underserved neighborhoods, poor health behaviors, lack of family wealth and other resources, and perhaps worst of all, a lack of hope for the future. Revisiting WHO's definition of health then, it's obvious that human beings faced with these conditions are not experiencing health. It is also clear that inequities created through collaborative efforts created these social determinants with the help of politics, along with policies created and followed by both private and public goods-and-service providers. Hence, there is a need for collective impact initiatives to co-create health equity that are both generative and adaptive.

Note: There are many other examples of how multi-sector collaborative efforts have contributed to health inequities, however exploring them is not the purpose of this book. For a deeper dive into political determinants of health, please consider reading The Political Determinants of Health, *by Daniel E. Dawes.*

Despite many definitions and explanations, I still hear people ask, "Yes, but what *really is* health equity?" The same thing used to happen in the literal part of my brain when I heard this question as when asked, "What is collaboration?" People want to understand what health equity looks like. They also want to know what collaboration looks like. Theoretically, we can use the right words to explain it, but practically it is a concept that requires co-laboring with adaptive and generative leadership for all of us to see what collaboration in pursuit of health equity *look like* together.

The reality of health equity is something we have not yet witnessed together in this country. So, we have to first see it in our minds, agree on what we see, and co-create the vision. How will you participate in this collective? Everything a society accomplishes begins at the individual level.

For those who prefer concrete examples, I welcome you to sit with the discomfort of not having health equity. Embrace the challenge of making the vision a reality while knowing that health equity will exist when every human being has the opportunity to pursue total well-being without obstacles created by systemic dishonesty, biases, or injustices that hinder the pursuit of the opportunity.

And to my colleagues who'll ask, "How do you measure this vision?" I'll respond, "When *every* human being has the opportunity to pursue total well-being without obstacles created by dishonesty, biases, or injustices that hinder the pursuit of the opportunity, the measure of health equity will be fulfilled."

This vision and its measurement are enormous undertakings. They require being rooted in compassion. It is compassion that allows for conscious collaboration.

Why Do We Need to Care About the Health Equity Cause?

When I first entered the health space as a well-being coach, I did so with my heart. I wanted to see that everyone I came into contact with had access to the knowledge and techniques that could help them improve the quality of their lives. I firmly believed then and still believe that living on purpose is something that is best done when you have the best health, mainly because you have the energy to do so; you are not distracted by diseases.

Because it is a passion of mine to see people live on purpose, I also want to see everyone do so while being healthy. Yes, those are the idealistic and altruistic aspects of me but a business mind coexists with those attributes in me and it recognizes the purpose of business: economic gain.

But is economic gain all there is? The purpose of business should be expanded to include altruistic ideals. Business—and economic gain—doesn't have to be a zero-sum game. Business, and the art of exchange, is ready to change for the better. It can start with you.

There are some for-profit businesses where the well-being of community is naturally built into their profit motive. The best example of this is a hospital. But there are many other businesses where such a natural fit may not be as apparent, but a connection to community well-being exists. A good example of that is Kroger's Bringing Hope to the Table program in support of food banks and its partnership with Feed America to ensure that American families in need have enough to eat.

It's necessary now to examine the costs of when there is a lack of health equity.

The Costs of Health Inequity

Karen M. Anderson and Steve Olson, reporting the results of a workshop titled "The Private Sector as a Catalyst for Health Equity and a Vibrant Economy" wrote, "The Organisation for Economic Cooperation and Development (OECD), the World Bank, and the World Economic Forum all now proclaim that equality and economic growth go hand in hand, that health, education, and economic security benefit not just individuals but the economy as a whole."[7]

Economic growth is limited, and I would argue stunted, because the people most impacted by inequities are not able to significantly contribute to the economy's growth by way of filling very needed employment gaps and consumption. When the cost of correcting health disparities emerges in discussion, an immediate "go to" for many is the cost of healthcare provided by medical facilities, supported by insurance companies, and subsidized by the government. Isolating health in this manner creates the challenge of seeing how inequities in health economically impacts all businesses in all sectors.

As a reminder, the definition of health was given as going beyond freedom from disease and infirmity, and being in a state of complete physical, mental, and social wellness. Additionally, the visual in chapter two demonstrated that whole health is of comprised 40 percent social factors (education, job status, family/social support, income, and commu-

7   https://www.nap.edu/catalog/23529/the-private-sector-as-a-catalyst-for-health-equity-and-a-vibrant-economy

nity safety), 30 percent behavioral factors (tobacco use, diet and exercise, alcohol use, and sexual activity), 20 percent healthcare factors (access to care and quality of care), and 10 percent environmental factors (air quality, access to nutritious foods, pure water, good sanitation). Further support of the full meaning of health was supported in research conducted by Gallup.[8] Their well-being research showed the five elements of health: career well-being, social well-being, financial well-being, physical well-being, and community well-being.

8   Rath, T. & Harther, J. (2014). Well-being: Five essential elements. Gallup Inc., NY

Total Health & Well-being:
Social Determinants of Health and
Gallup Well-being Elements

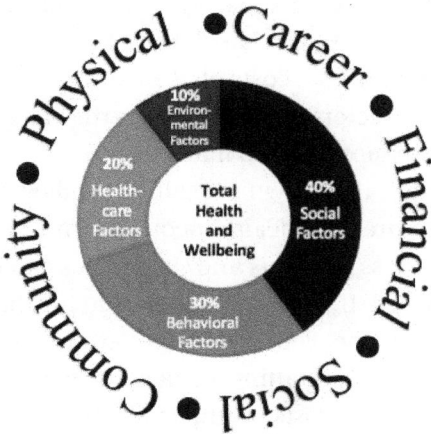

Image created by Sheron Brown, Ph.D.

When health is viewed in totality, it becomes easier to see how the cost of disparities extends beyond the cost of healthcare provided by medical facilities, supported by insurance companies, and subsidized by the government.

Neither hospitals nor health insurance companies pay for health aspects such as lack of education or the gaps in employability (social factors), but for-profit companies do both directly and indirectly.

A thoughtful analysis of the Total Health and Well-being pie reveals that all factors that lead to good health are interrelated. And this fact drives home the point that costs of its inequity financially impacts all sectors. It also supports the value of a multi-sector approach to make health equity real. For example, if you own a locally owned business or an entrepreneur, health inequities impact your business—less products and/or services can or will be purchased. If you own a car dealership, health inequities impact your business—fewer cars are sold. If you own a staffing agency, less people are employable. The costs of employee productivity due to illness-related absenteeism impacts every type of businesses.

Nonprofits and government agencies continue to see costs increase annually as they work tirelessly to address social ills in their communities. This requires them to seek more funding annually through donations, grants, and tax dollars. Yet the burden of addressing social ills should not rest with the public sector alone. As quoted earlier in this book, "no single organization is responsible for any major social problem, nor can any single organization cure it. [...] Social problems arise from the interplay of governmental and commercial activities, not only from the behavior of social sector organizations. As a result, complex problems can be solved only by a cross-sector coalition that engages those outside the nonprofit sector."[9]

Diversity, Equity, and Inclusion and Health Equity Are Related

Heightened racial tensions have increased the focus on Diversity, Equity and Inclusion (DEI) in the workplace. Many organizations now have whole departments and chief executives whose sole focus is to ensure fairness across groups to include all identities such as gender, age, race, sexual orientation, cultures, abilities, religion, and more. These "in-house" efforts are very important for the growth of organizations. Research has shown that well executed DEI efforts influence innovation, performance, financial results, and other good aspects of business. The inward focus of DEI on the part of organizations is critical for business growth as is

---

9 https://ssir.org/articles/entry/collective_impact

health equity, with its outward focus. The two are interrelated.

Being mindful about removing obstacles to fairness through policies and practices influences health equity in a variety of ways. For example, when thought is given to how to expand growth opportunities to low wage earners, and the same employees eventually grow in skills and earning, the result is an impact on SDoH factors such as income, job status, and access to care. Likewise, being mindful of how business contributes to health equity externally in community and society at large is equally important because community well-being impacts everyone. Since the COVID-19 pandemic, that fact is evident.

I would be remiss if I did not bring your awareness to another layer of issues that make co-creating health equity a challenge. Solving the problem of health inequity through collaboration requires an understanding of the relationship of childhood trauma to adult health. Science has proven that traumas suffered during childhood are significant indicators of a person's lifelong health profile. The Adverse Childhood Experiences (ACEs) Study was published in 1999 by the American Journal of Preventive Medicine. Although the proof it offered met with resistance early on, it is now accepted as a useful tool and is used by teachers, social workers, physicians, and others who work to remove barriers to health. The Centers for Disease Control and Prevention gives an overview of this important study at http://www.cdc.gov/violenceprevention/aces. This layer of complexity further elucidates why a multi-sector approach to eliminating health inequities is paramount.

> *Note: It is absolutely necessary to acknowledge the constructs of race and racism along with their systemic, structural, and institutional implications in any discussion about equity—particularly in the United States. These constructs greatly contribute to the inequities we are currently facing as a society. A deep understanding of these factors benefits the discussion of health equity. However, the focus of this book is conscious collaboration, and I feel it's worth it to share how racism does impact health equity. The following visual shows the direct relationship between racism and health and well-being.*

Health Disparities are Driven by Social and Economic Inequities

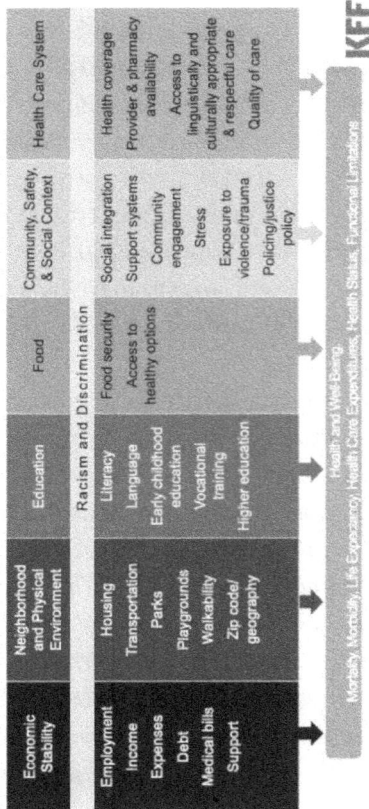

Economic Stability	Neighborhood and Physical Environment	Education	Food	Community, Safety, & Social Context	Health Care System
Employment	Housing	Literacy	Food security	Social integration	Health coverage
Income	Transportation	Language	Access to healthy options	Support systems	Provider & pharmacy availability
Expenses	Parks	Early childhood education		Community engagement	Access to linguistically and culturally appropriate & respectful care
Debt	Playgrounds	Vocational training		Stress	Quality of care
Medical bills	Walkability	Higher education		Exposure to violence/trauma	
Support	Zip code/geography			Policing/justice policy	

Racism and Discrimination

Health and Well Being

Mortality, Morbidity, Life Expectancy, Health Care Expenditures, Health Status, Functional Limitations

KFF

Note: For a deeper dive on the connection between racism and health inequities, please consider searching the internet to find a number of extremely informative books and resources. A few initial sources to consider are the Racial Equity Institute, Common Health Action, and the Health Equity Tracker.

Health Equity Dollars and Sense

Inequities cost. One of the key findings in an article titled, "The Business Case For Racial Equity: A Strategy For Growth," by Ani Turner indicates that nationally "There is a potential economic gain of $135 billion per year if racial disparities in health are eliminated, including $93 billion in excess medical care costs and $42 billion in untapped productivity."[10] A mathematical breakdown of how that impacts any local region would undoubtedly show billions in lost dollars to your community.

For example, Tim Dutton, CEO of Unite Pinellas in Pinellas County, Florida shared: "The economy of Pinellas County could have been $3.6 billion stronger in 2016 if its racial gaps in income had

---

10 https://altarum.org/RacialEquity2018

been closed. Similarly, the economy of Hillsborough County would have been $11.3 billion greater."[11] If you are in that region, what does that mean for your organization? If you are not in Pinellas County, what share of the national numbers belong to your business? Would the leaders in your for-profit organization want to capture those dollars? Of course they would. To capture the value lost, all sectors must engage in making health equity a reality.

Health equity is more than economics; it is about total well-being, both individual and community, yet an important element of that totality is financial. Therefore, for the sake of well-being in every community in the United States, health equity should be everyone's goal. The success of health equity, or costs of health inequity, always impacts business, regardless of sector.

Yes, the pursuit of health equity is idealistic, but it is an altruistic ideal that benefits us all. This is where my plan for The Conscious Collaboration Pathway™ comes into play. It is an approach that allows the public and private sectors to engage in collective impact initiatives that will make health equity efforts cost effective and sustainable while improving communities and the lives of individuals.

---

11 Personal email on February 25, 2020

A Quick Note About
Systems Thinking

*All things appear and disappear because of the
concurrence of causes and conditions. Nothing
ever exists entirely alone; everything is in
relation to everything else.*

— The Buddha

C3 80

Discussing the connections between collective
impact, health equity, and conscious collaboration
without addressing 'systems thinking' would be
a lost opportunity. Thinking in systems is a topic
that is respected, but it is rare that I see it in action.
Systems thinking is used to solve social challenges, and the approach promises to yield sustained
impact if used.

A pioneer in the field of systems thinking, Donel-
la H. Meadows wrote about it in *Thinking in Systems:
A Primer*. According to her definition, a system is "a
set of elements or parts that is coherently organized
and interconnected in a pattern or structure that
produces a characteristic set of behaviors, often
classified as its function or purpose" (Meadows,

2008).[12] Systems thinking is an approach to solutioning that considers the connections between everything. Good leaders are aware that within an organization it is best to use this approach to solve problems instead of creating isolated departmental solutions that can result in problems for a connected department. All parts work together. Such is the case with organizations across sectors, yet initiatives to address social ills via a 'systems thinking' approach are rare.

A critical point that ought to be internalized by leaders in all sectors is repeated often in this book. Remember, "no single organization is responsible for any major social problem, nor can any single organization cure it. [...] The problem with relying on the isolated impact of individual organizations is further compounded by the isolation of the nonprofit sector. Social problems arise from the interplay of governmental and commercial activities, not only from the b ehavior of social sector organizations. As a result, complex problems can be solved only by a cross-sector coalition that engages those outside the nonprofit sector."[13]

---

12   Meadows, D.H. (2008). Thinking in Systems: A Primer. p. 188. Chelsea Green Publishing, VT.

13   https://ssir.org/articles/entry/collective_impact

Consider this graphic that shows simplified interplay between commercial, governmental, and social sectors.

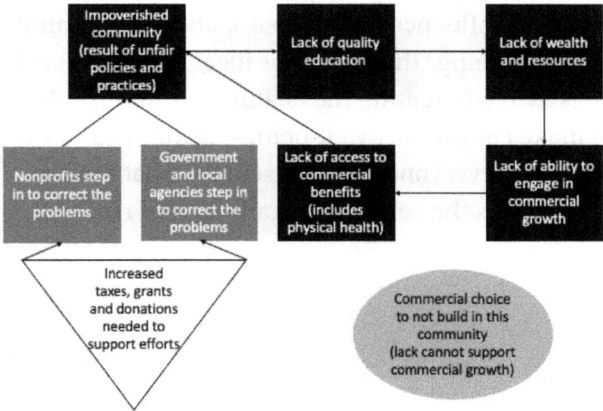

Image created by Sheron Brown, Ph.D.

Ideally, multi-sector groups within a community would engage in this exercise to determine what the collective impact is of their isolated actions on their community. As a result, unintended impacts on each other and the community at large would emerge and present opportunities to co-create whole system solutions that result in positive collective impact.

As stated in the repeated quote, complex problems such as inequities in health require a multi-sector approach in order to create sustainable solutions that have collective impact. For-profit practices influence social health, and thus community well-being. Therefore, it is ideal for all sectors to engage in co-creating the healing of communities to make community well-being—health equity—a reality for everyone. The Conscious Collaboration Pathway™ is the solution for gaining that reality.

What is The Conscious Collaboration Pathway™?

Consciousness is a concept that can sound esoteric, but all it really means is caring.

— Tony Robbins

୨୨

A good practice for your brain whenever you are about to try something different or new is to remember the four stages of change.[14] Introducing new behavior can sometimes be challenging, mainly because your brain likes the comfort and certainty associated with doing what is familiar. New behaviors associated with new learning sends a warning signal to the brain that something is wrong and potentially harmful. This threat response can cause you to want to give up, and to do so with what sounds like justified reasoning.

Preparing for the Pathway

Engaging in collaboration is not harmful to you or anyone else. Logically you are aware of this but

---

14 Scott and Jaffe, "Survive and Thrive in Times of Change" https://www.researchgate.net/publication/235284220_Resistance_to_organizational_change_The_role_of_cognitive_and_affective_processes

knowing that the brain can lure you with clever deceit in the name of protection, it is ideal to arm yourself with a tool as a reminder. As you prepare to learn about and employ The Conscious Collaboration Pathway™, I offer you a reminder of what your brain may experience—the four stages of change.

The Four Stages of Change

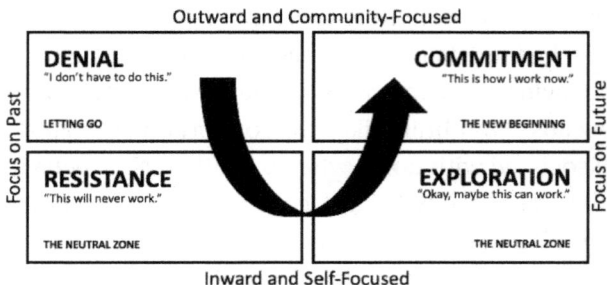

Outward and Community-Focused

DENIAL		COMMITMENT
"I don't have to do this."		"This is how I work now."
LETTING GO		THE NEW BEGINNING
RESISTANCE		EXPLORATION
"This will never work."		"Okay, maybe this can work."
THE NEUTRAL ZONE		THE NEUTRAL ZONE

Focus on Past   Focus on Future

Inward and Self-Focused

Source: Scott & Jaffe, "Survive and Thrive in Times of Change"

As you make your way into The Conscious Collaboration Pathway™, perhaps between steps two through five, you'll experience denial. Be aware of thoughts that may sound like, "Why am I even doing this?" or "I don't have to do this." This is the first stage of change. Push through it.

Next, if you hear your thoughts say, "This will never work," or, "What we've been doing is just fine," know that your brain is in the stage of resistance. Your brain feels uncomfortable with the new behavior being presented, but if you acknowledge what is happening, you can and will move to the third stage of exploration. It is possible that somewhere between steps five through seven of The Conscious Collaboration Pathway™ you may have thoughts that indicate your brain is beginning to feel safe and open to exploring. Your thoughts may sound like, "Maybe this can work," or, "This is possible."

Finally, your brain will arrive at the commitment stage of change. Here is where it feels confident that you can succeed and is ready for a new beginning. You will arrive here at the final step of The Conscious Collaboration Pathway™.

Now armed with the reminder of how your brain may respond and a tool to guide your thinking, you are prepared for The Conscious Collaboration Pathway™.

The Conscious Collaboration Pathway™

In the Buddhist tradition, there is a concept called the Noble Eightfold Path. It is a set of principles that, when incorporated into one's lifestyle with earnestness, collectively contribute to eliminating chaos and suffering created by the mind. Similarly, the purpose of The Conscious Collaboration Pathway™ is to provide an approach that, when applied to collaboration effort and adhered to with good intentions, eliminates the concerns that arise with the thought of competition. Application of The Conscious Collaboration Pathway™ advances collective efforts shared by multi-sector stakeholders to achieve collective impact.

The eight steps of Conscious Collaboration Pathway™ follow:

Step 1: Enter the exploration to collaborate with a win-win mindset.

Decide at the onset that when a collaboration agreement is reached, all organizations involved will experience the win-win effect, and all people who personally engage in the efforts will be whole throughout the process. This first step opens the pathway with being conscious, or mindful, of how everyone engages.

Step 2: Share your organization's mission, vision, and values.

Take the time to explain your mission, vision, and values—the reasons why they are and what they are, and to share stories that exemplify or amplify their meaning. This step allows you to deeply know your potential collaborator, contribute to determining if they are a good fit, and it helps you to continue to be conscious along the pathway.

Step 3: Identify connections and commonalities.

This step may require digital tools or traditional poster-sized paper and markers. During this step you create a list or a visual map to display how and where all parties' mission, vision, and values overlap. Doing this will strengthen the ability to generate win-win goals once you co-create a collective impact initiative. Additionally, identifying connections will allow you to excavate and share hearts in your work.

Step 4: Determine the collective impact and outcomes.

At this stage, the decision makers representing a cross-sector group of organizations are beginning to shape the initiative. It is important that the initiative helps, while unleashing the power within those being helped to be equipped to eventually help themselves. Be mindful about how the for-profit collaborator can leverage their strengths. This step involves applying 'systems thinking' principles and creating a logic model (like a roadmap) to guide the work involved in the initiative.

Step 5: Decide and agree what a win looks like for each entity.

Because each organization has its own mission, vision, and values, a win may not look the same for everyone. Each organization has other stakeholders to report to (e.g. board members, shareholders, supervisors, etc.), and so it is important to be clear about what everyone needs for the collaboration to work successfully. Again, this step cultivates an awareness of the needs of others.

Step 6: Document the rules of engagement.

In all exchanges and interactions between people, some version of an agreement creates a foundation for a healthy relationship, especially when parties enter with good intentions for the wholeness of all. Depending on the organizations involved, the collaboration may call for an agreement ranging anywhere from an informal charter to a formal legally binding contract. This will help with staying focused on the work and the win with limited confusion.

Step 7: Establish goals and success measures.

All ventures of good quality have goals and measurements. The information generated in step four will shape the goals and metrics. Additionally, include milestones and agreed upon dates when you all will gather again to discuss progress, create a plan to remove obstacles, and share wins. This step will keep everyone mindful while creating the path and being on the journey.

Step 8: Plan how you will celebrate milestones.

It is easy to see progress and keep pressing forward for more, but it is important to be deliberate about stopping to celebrate the wins. Celebrating together enhances your network, strengthens your psychology and attracts more wins[15]. This step will support your conscious (caring) collaboration and joy throughout the process of creating positive and collective impact in your community.

The Conditions for Success

Now that you know what Conscious Collaboration Pathway™ is, you should also be aware of the conditions that will cultivate a collaborative environment. Collective impact by way of Conscious Collaboration Pathway™ is necessary to eliminate health inequities; however, unless all entities involved accept these conditions, all impacts will be compromised.

Also, in the Buddhist tradition, there is a set of conditions referred to as The Four Noble Truths. They set the foundation to make The Eightfold Path possible. Similarly, the following conditions are the

---

15 https://www.inc.com/bill-carmody/3-reasons-celebrating-your-many-accomplishments-is-critical-to-your-success.html

foundation for Conscious Collaboration Pathway™ and must be embraced before moving forward to create collective impact. They are the following:

1. Establish in your mind that the collaborative effort you enter will align with your work and your mission. Anything that detracts from your North Star is invaluable and energy draining.

2. Be willing to co-create a common energizing agenda and a system for shared metrics. Without a common energizing agenda your initiative will fizzle. Without shared metrics there is no accountability or sustained actions.

3. Accept that regular communication is a part of the process. Communication builds relationships, fosters trust, and contributes to motivated action. Regular meetings will be necessary, but to avoid meetings for the sake of meetings, engage a facilitator.

4. Know that a supporting organization is needed to ensure a successful collaboration with a structured process. The supporting organization focuses attention, creates a sense of urgency, frames issues to present opportunities and challenges, and mediates conflict. The supporting organization also serves as a project

manager, data manager, and facilitator. Again, this condition contributes greatly to the success of the collaboration.[16]

The Conscious Collaboration Pathway™ and its eight steps and four conditions for success, while not Buddhist practices, are similar to The Noble Eightfold Path and The Four Noble Truths. In the ancient tradition, the path and truths help the individual end suffering that is created by the mind to improve the overall conditions of mankind. Similarly, Conscious Collaboration Pathway™ and its four conditions for success help individuals enter a collaborative relationship with mental ease toward the goal of improving the conditions of mankind.

It is time for multiple sectors in our society to move away from isolated impacts to fully embrace collective impacts. This change can feel like a big one, but there are small steps you can take that will lead to the bold actions that yield impact.

---

16 https://ssir.org/articles/entry/collective_impact

What Can You Do Now?

Once we start to act, hope is everywhere.
So instead of looking for hope, look for action.
Then, and only then, hope will come.

— Greta Thunberg

୧୭ ୨୦

After reading this book, will you take action? I hope so...I want you to act! Regardless of the position you hold or the organization you work for or the sector you represent, there are small steps you can take now that will lead to big actions and collective impacts. Here is a list of actions that outline multiple entry points to support advancing collective impact in your community.

Join TBHC Collaborate
What is it and how will it help?

TBHC Collaborate is a digital platform designed to help people who work in nonprofits and agencies that address the Social Determinants of Health (SDoH) factors. The platform serves as a hub for them to network, share and explore collaboration opportunities, share events, and identify funding opportunities where they are able to collaborate. The platform is also a place for Foundations and other donors to share funding opportunities, particularly those that encourage collaboration.

Joining TBHC Collaborate will increase opportunities to engage in collective impact, use donor dollars wisely, leverage organizational strengths among smaller nonprofits, and reduce redundancies across a region.

Who is it for?

This opportunity is for people who work in the following organization types:

- Nonprofits
- Local Agencies
- Community Based Organizations
- Local government
- Funders

How may I access it?

Access TBHC Collaborate for your iPhone.

Access TBHC Collaborate for your Android.

Access TBHC Collaborate for your desktop.

Join a TBHC Impact Council

What is it and how will it help?

TBHC has three mission-aligned Impact Councils: (1) Awareness Impact Council; (2) Building Capacity Impact Council; and the (3) Collaboration Impact Council. The members represent a wide range of organizations in the community. In addition to building authentic relationships and exploring opportunities to collaborate with each other, members of each council work together to create networking and learning opportunities for the community to support TBHC's member-driven mission to promote and advance health equity through awareness, building capacity, and fostering collaboration.

Joining an Impact Council will allow you to network and grow with other community leaders as you advance community well-being together. Your efforts will educate and inspire all who engage in Impact Council experiences and events and contribute to promoting collective impact.

Who is it for?

This opportunity is for people who work in the following organization types:

- Nonprofits
- Local Agencies

- Community Based Organizations
- Local government
- Funders
- Businesses

How can I access it?

Use the QR code to access details for signing up for the next monthly Impact Council meeting.

Become a TBHC Member or Connector

What is it and how will it help?

Traditionally, TBHC membership has been by organization, and connectors are individual people. Both routes allow you or your organization to stay informed and hold the title of health equity leader.

Joining TBHC as a member and/or connector supports our movement of promoting and advancing health equity through collective impact, because as you know in movements, numbers matter.

Who is it for?

This opportunity is for people who work in the following organization types:

- Nonprofits
- Local Agencies
- Community Based Organizations
- Local government
- Funders
- Businesses

How can I access it?

Use the QR code below to sign up your organization as a member or yourself as a connector.

Become a Donor

How will it help?

As a donor, your dollars support the mission of TBHC to promote and advance health equity through increasing awareness, building capacity, and fostering collaboration. Your dollars will support our programs that encourage cross-sector collaboration for collective impact.

Who is it for?

In addition to community members, this opportunity is for people who work in the following organization types:

- Individuals
- Nonprofits
- Local Agencies
- Community Based Organizations
- Local government
- Funders
- Businesses

How can I donate?

Donations to TBHC are tax deductible. To learn about becoming a donor, use the following QR code to contact TBHC.

If you believe your donation size warrants a conversation, please contact TBHC directly.

Become a Sponsor

What is sponsorship and how will it help?

TBHC views sponsorships as financial support for specific programming such as for the TBHC Collaborate, TBHC Impact Councils, and additional programs not shared in this book. (Please contact TBHC to learn more.)

Your sponsorship will support a platform where users in the SDoH space share opportunities to collaborate on initiatives, connect with others who do similar work, and find opportunities to share access to funding. Sponsorships also support the creation of learning spaces and experiences that help multi-sector leaders identify and eliminate barriers to health equity on jobsites.

Who is it for?

This opportunity is for the following organization types:

- Nonprofits
- Local Agencies
- Community Based Organizations
- Local government
- Funders
- Businesses

How can I become a sponsor?

To learn about becoming a sponsor, use the following QR code to contact TBHC.

Become a Partner

What is partnership and how will it help?

Corporate responsibility, social impact, and equity. These concepts are essential elements for the sustainability of a 21st century company and a healthy democracy. Organizations committed to equity demonstrate their belief through action. They take actions like examining and revising policies and practices to elevate equity in the workplace. A step further includes examining policies that positively impact health equity in the workplace and influence the well-being of diverse groups within the organization. Such commitment is commendable. Still, there are organizations that have a strong desire to impact societal well-being and equity in the local community they serve, but do not have the bandwidth to do so because their desire may not align with operational and performance goals. Partnering with TBHC gives your organization the opportunity to accomplish your desire to impact societal well-being by allowing TBHC to serve as an extension to the community of your internal commitment to equity.

Your partnership will help TBHC reach three shared goals: 1) creating more awareness around health equity; 2) building capacity to increase health equity; and, 3) fostering collaboration to advance health equity across multi-sector organizations, all to ensure that we close the economic and health gaps in our communities and to ensure resources are utilized more efficiently.

Who is it for?

This opportunity is for the following organization types:

- Funders
- Businesses

How can I access it?

To learn about becoming a partner, use the following QR code to contact TBHC.

Share this Book

How will it help?

The purpose of this book is to spread the message of The Conscious Collaboration Pathway™ and its importance to community well-being. Sharing this book spreads the message across communities, advances health equity, and contributes to improving community health physically, socially, and economically.

Who is it for?

In addition to your colleagues, this book is for people who work in the following organization types:

- Nonprofits
- Local Agencies
- Community Based Organizations
- Local government
- Funders
- Businesses

How can they access copies of this book to share?
Copies of this book can be accessed by using the QR code below. Capture the link to email five to ten people and ask them to share this book.

Contact Dr. Brown for a Conscious Collaboration Pathway™ Workshop

Why, what is the workshop, and how will it help?

The Conscious Collaboration Pathway™ workshop is an extension of this book. During the workshop, participants gain deeper insights about the process through engaging in practical application of each step.

If you are part of a nonprofit, the process will help you identify your organization's unique value to the community in order to eliminate the fear of competition, create opportunities to demonstrate deeper impact to donors, and maximize learner dollars with the act of collaboration.

Those people employed by for-profit companies should know that The Conscious Collaboration Pathway™ helps you determine how best to engage in collective impact given your organization's specific industry and identify social impact investments that align with your organization's place within the societal system.

Who is it for?

This workshop is for people who work in the following organization types:

- Nonprofits
- Local Agencies
- Community Based Organizations
- Local government
- Funders
- Businesses

How can you access workshop information?

Use the link in the QR to connect with Dr. Brown and inquire about a workshop.

Which action(s) will you take toward collective impact today?

_____

_____

_____

_____

_____

_____

_____

_____

_____

_____

_____

_____

_____

_____

The Conscious Collaboration Pathway™

About the Author

Photo credit: Brandi Image Photography

Sheron Brown, Ph.D. is a woman of purpose, driven by vision. In her current role as executive director of the Tampa Bay Health Collaborative (TBHC), Dr. Brown has a keen focus on bringing individuals and organizations together to work collaboratively towards health equity. Her innovative and modern approaches to establishing partnerships and encouraging resource-sharing have been recognized by *Tampa Bay Times and St. Pete Catalyst.*

Prior to joining the Tampa Bay Healthcare Collaborative, Dr. Brown founded and operated a private health and wellness practice, Sweet Eden by

Sheron. Through her company, Dr. Brown served as a wellness educator, consultant and coach to schools, school leaders, and women of color who struggle with chronic disease. Today, she uses her passion for harmony and health equity to help all parties she connects with via TBHC to leverage their identity individually and collectively, as well as embrace their personal and collective power to bring about transformation within the community.

www.ingramcontent.com/pod-product-compliance
Lightning Source LLC
Chambersburg PA
CBHW051038030426
42336CB00015B/2934